TUMBLEWEEDS
ROUNDUP!
BY
TOM K. RYAN

A FAWCETT GOLD MEDAL BOOK

Fawcett Publications, Inc., Greenwich, Connecticut

WELL!? WHAT ARE YOU GAWKING AT?!

THERE'S A PERFECTLY LOGICAL EXPLANATION!

THE PLACE IS FULL OF FLIES AND I CAN'T FIND MY SWATTER!

"'ELLIE SUE NEEDS ME!' CRIED BRET HARDY, LEAPING INTO THE SADDLE! 'AWAY, THUNDER, BOY!' AND THE GREAT GLEAMING STALLION, EVERY RIPPLING SINEW STRAINING, HURTLED FORTH WITH ALL THE UNLEASHED POWER AND FURY OF A LIGHTNING BOLT!"

PWT!

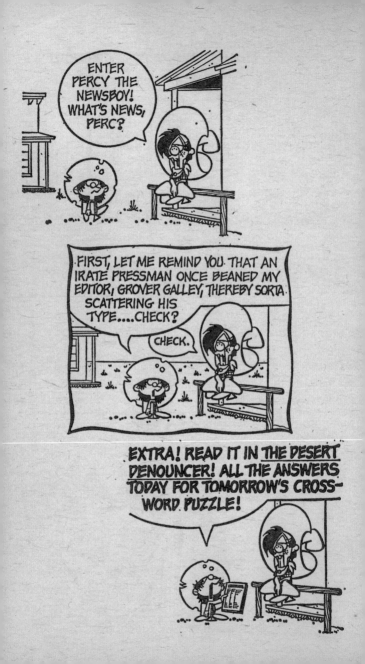

S'MATTER, PERCY?

IT'S FLAKE CITY

GROVER, MY EDITOR'S ON ONE OF HIS DREAM-UP-A-WEIRD-HEADLINE-THEN-LOOK-FOR-A-STORY-TO-GO-WITH-IT KICKS.

SUCH AS?

"HORSELESS RUSTLER STRIKES. RANCHERS BAFFLED!"

CHEER UP. IT COULD BE WORSE

DESERT DENOUNCER

IT IS.

LOOK, FATHER. LIMPID LIZARD GAVE ME SOME OF HIS FINGERNAIL CLIPPINGS TO REMEMBER HIM BY.

GAD! SUCH LAVISH GENEROSITY!

WHY, WITH A BIT OF INGENUITY, DEAR, YOU CAN BE THE PROUD POSSESSOR OF A GENUINE CLOD CLAW NECKLACE!

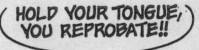

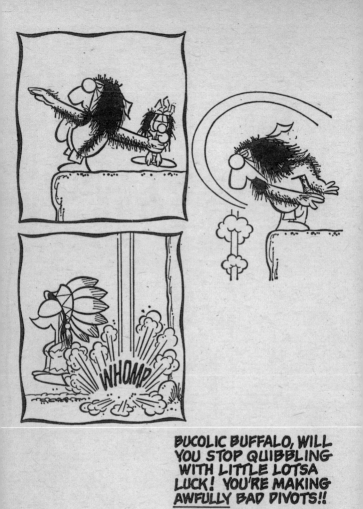

WHOMP

BUCOLIC BUFFALO, WILL YOU STOP QUIBBLING WITH LITTLE LOTSA LUCK! YOU'RE MAKING AWFULLY BAD DIVOTS!!

"HUSBAND HUNTER'S HANDBOOK.
If you must propose to HIM,
Future Bride, be sure to do so
with <u>extreme</u> tact."

"HUSBAND HUNTERS' HANDBOOK"

"A hint, Future Bride: Some men are attracted to women of exotic and mysterious races. Maybe HE is one of them!"

NO, HILDEGARD, ODDLY ENOUGH I HAVE NO TEA LEAVES ON ME, NOR, STRANGE AS IT MAY SEEM, NO CRYSTAL BALL OR EVEN A OUIJA BOARD.

NO SWEAT, DOLL! I'LL WING IT, AS WE GYPSIES SAY! I'LL TELL YOUR FORTUNE BY GOING INTO A DEEP, DEEP **TRANCE!**

I AM NOW IN A DEEP TRANCE! I AM GETTING A PICTURE! AH! IT IS YOUR **FUTURE!:** A CUTE LOCAL GIRL IS WITH YOU! SHE'S PART GYPSY, PART CIVILIAN! HARK! I HEAR WEDDING BELLS! YOU ARE BEING SHOWERED WITH RICE!...

HEADIN' 'EM OFF AT THE PASS YOU ARE NOT.

SCRIBBLE
SCRIBBLE
SCRIBBLE
SCRIBBLE
SCRIBBLE
SCRIBBLE

ODE TO MY SHAVEN HEAD

WHERE ONCE SNUG DANDRUFF LAY BY DAY
AND TICKS IN MOONLIT GLADES DID PLAY,
NOW O'ER THY DESERT WASTE OF SKIN
A CHILL WIND SWEEPS FROM NAPE TO CHIN.

ALAS, DEFOLIATED BEAN,
YOU'VE MADE THE YUL AND TELLY SCENE,
AND NIGH THY BARREN, HAUNTED DOME
A HOMESICK COMB SULKS IN THE GLOAM.

FACE IT, POETRY FREAKS
...A NEW GIANT LOOMS
ON THE HORIZON.

SCRIBBLE
SCRIBBLE
SCRIBBLE

CITIZENS OF GRIMY GULCH!: ON THIS, THE **17½th ANNIVERSARY** OF OUR COMMUNITY, I DECLARE A **WEEK-LONG FIESTA** IN HONOR OF THE STERLING QUALITIES THAT HAVE MADE IT RENOWNED!

SO, REJOICE AND EXULT!

JUDGE FRUMP'S COURT

LET'S MAKE **FRUMP WEEK** A MEMORABLE ONE!

VERILY, DERE'S NUTTIN' SO HELPLESS AS A CHILD SICKIE. MAYHAPS I SHOULD WAFT ALOFT A PRAYER FER DA TOT...

BIG BOSS IN DA SKY: IF YOUSE'LL LAY A MIRACLE ON ME BABY BRUDDER, I PROMISE DAT IF I EVER GOES BACK T' CHOICH, I'LL PUT IN DA COLLECTION BASKET ALL DA SCRATCH I'VE TOOK OUTA IT. AMEN.

HIC!

WELL, 'WEEDS, IT'S TIME I GOT BACK TO THE GALLOWS CIRCUIT! I'M BOOKED FOR A ONE-DAWN STAND IN NAUSEA JUNCTION, A MATINEE IN HOGTOWN, AND A TREE LIMB GIG IN ZITSVILLE!

AS WE SAY IN THE TRADE: A DANGLE A DAY KEEPS THE BLUES AWAY!...ONCE A TROUPER ALWAYS A TROUPER! THE SHOW MUST GO ON!

GRIMY GULCH
POP. 49

BREAK A ROPE

GRIMY GULCH
POP. 49

CHIEF, OUR CRITICAL BUSINESS SLUMP REMINDS ME OF A STORY I READ IN A RECENT ISSUE OF "EXCAVATORS ILLUSTRATED"...

IN IT THIS MORTICIAN SMUGGLED A VAMPIRE INTO THE COUNTRY TO HELP STIMULATE HIS SAGGING ECONOMY...IT'S ENTITLED "THE TRANSYLVANIAN CONNECTION".

DISGUSTING

JUST FICTION, OF COURSE

CLAUDE CLAY
UNDERTAKER
YOU PLUG 'EM—I PLANT 'EM

SHUCKS

HAVE MORE FUN
WITH TUMBLEWEEDS